The Artistic Symphony

A simple guide to acrylic pour painting

Welcome to the world of acrylic pour painting, where vibrant colours dance freely across the canvas, creating mesmerizing patterns and captivating compositions. Whether you're a seasoned artist or a curious beginner, this book is your comprehensive guide to mastering the art of acrylic pour painting.

In the following chapters, we'll delve into the techniques, materials, and creative processes involved in acrylic pour painting. From understanding the basics of acrylics and mediums to experimenting with different pouring methods and styles, you'll discover how to unleash your creativity and express yourself through this dynamic and versatile medium.

So, grab your brushes, prepare your paints, and let's embark on a colourful journey into the captivating world of acrylic pour painting.

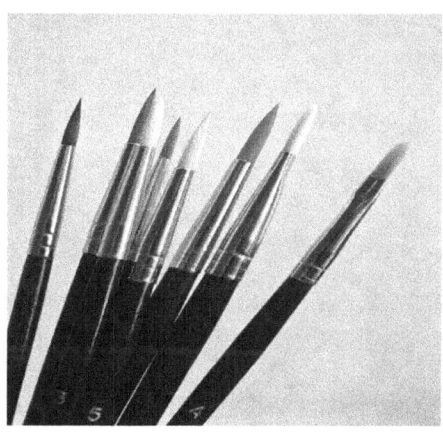

Chapter 1: Getting Started

1.1 Understanding Acrylic Paints and Mediums

Properties of acrylic paints

Types of acrylic mediums

Choosing the right materials for pouring

1.2 Preparing Your Workspace

Setting up a suitable work area

Gathering necessary tools and supplies

Preparing your canvas or surface

1.3 Basic Pouring Techniques

The flip cup method

The dirty pour technique

The swipe technique

The string pull technique

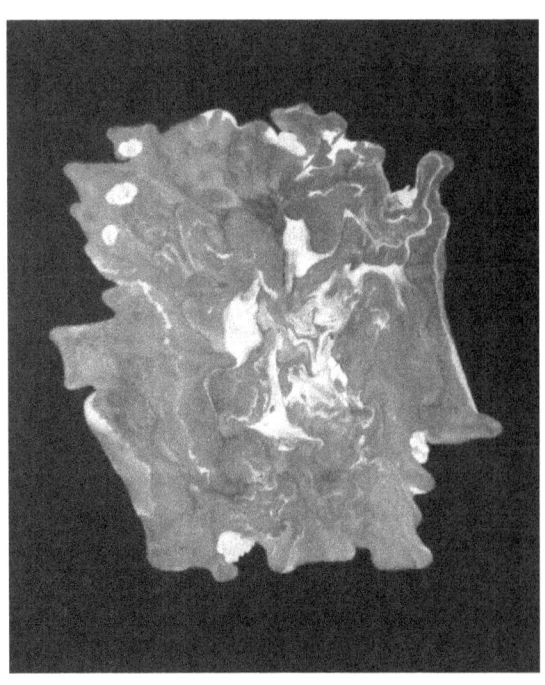

Chapter 2: Exploring Colour and Composition

2.1 Colour Theory for Pouring

Understanding colour mixing and blending

Creating harmonious colour schemes

Using colour psychology in your compositions

2.2 Composition and Design Principles

Exploring balance, contrast, and focal points

Creating dynamic compositions with negative space

Experimenting with different pouring styles for varied effects

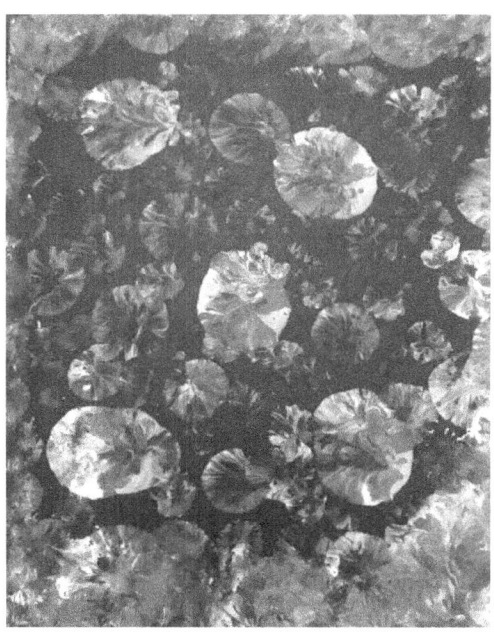

Chapter 3: Advanced Pouring Techniques

3.1 Layering and Cell Formation

Creating depth and dimension with layered pours

Understanding the science behind cell formation

Techniques for promoting cell formation in your paintings

3.2 Resin Finishes and Other Enhancements

Achieving a glossy, professional finish with resin

Incorporating additional elements like glitter or metallic leaf

Tips for varnishing and sealing your finished pieces

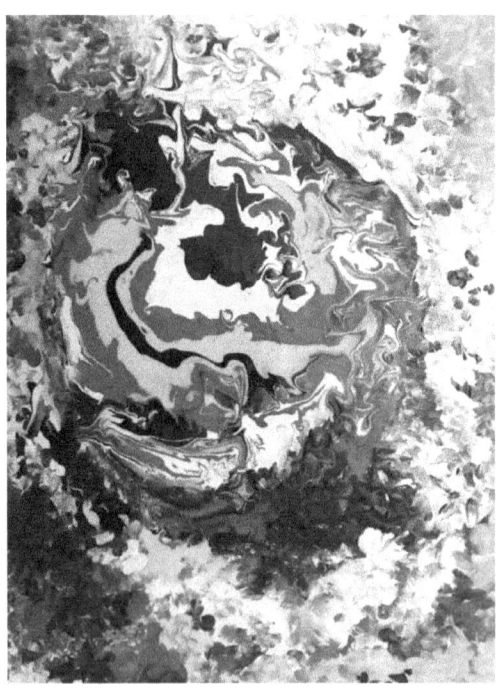

Chapter 4: Troubleshooting and Tips

4.1 Common Pouring Problems and Solutions

Dealing with cracking, crazing, or uneven drying

Preventing colour muddying and overmixing

Troubleshooting issues with cells or lacing

4.2 Tips and Tricks for Successful Pouring

Managing paint consistency for optimal flow

Experimenting with different pouring mediums and additives

Embracing experimentation and embracing happy accidents

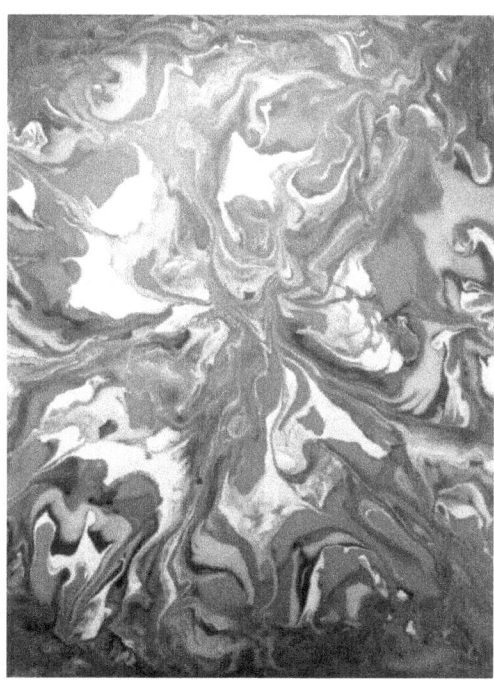

Chapter 5: Finding Your Style and Voice

5.1 Developing Your Personal Style

Exploring different artistic influences and inspirations

Experimenting with various techniques and approaches

Reflecting on your artistic journey and growth

5.2 Sharing Your Artwork

Building a portfolio of your work

Engaging with the acrylic pour painting community

Exploring opportunities for exhibitions and sales

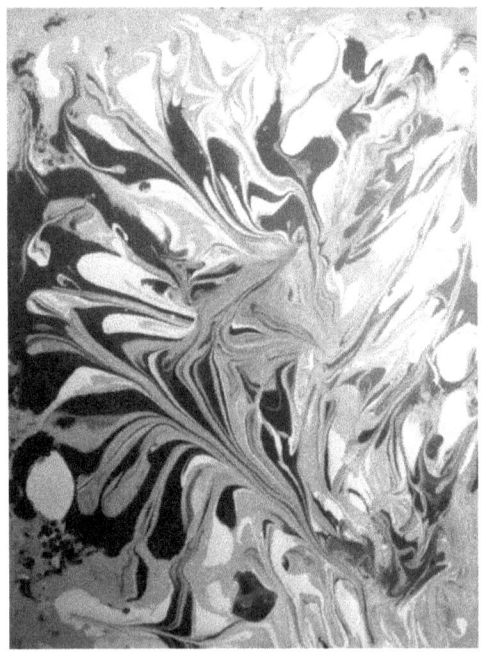

Chapter 1: Getting Started

Acrylic pour painting is a fascinating and exciting art form that involves pouring acrylic paint onto a canvas to create stunning abstract designs. Here are some steps to help you get started:

Gather Your Materials:

Acrylic paint: Choose a variety of colours that you want to use in your painting.

Pouring medium: This helps to thin the paint and improve flow, allowing for smooth pouring and blending.

Canvas: Pick a canvas or other painting surface to pour onto.

Cups and stir sticks: Use these to mix your paint and pouring medium.

Drop cloth or plastic sheet: Protect your work area from spills and drips.

Gloves: Keep your hands clean and protected from paint.

Prepare Your Workspace:

Lay down your drop cloth or plastic sheet to protect your work surface.

Set up your canvas on top of the protective covering.

Mix Your Paint:

In separate cups, mix your acrylic paint with the pouring medium. Start with a 1:1 ratio and adjust as needed for your desired consistency. You want the paint to be thin enough to pour easily but not too watery.

Preparing your workspace is crucial for a successful acrylic pour painting session. Here are some steps to ensure your area is ready:

Covering and Protection:

Lay down a protective covering such as a drop cloth, plastic sheet, or old newspapers to protect your work surface from spills, drips, and splatters.

Ensure that the covering extends beyond the edges of your work area to catch any stray paint.

Ventilation:

Acrylic paints and mediums can emit fumes, so it's essential to work in a well-ventilated area. Open windows and doors to allow for proper airflow.

If you're working in a space with limited ventilation, consider using a fan or wearing a respirator mask to reduce exposure to fumes.

Organize Your Materials:

Gather all the materials you'll need for your pour painting, including acrylic paints, pouring mediums, mixing cups, stir sticks, gloves, and your painting surface (canvas or board).

Arrange your materials within easy reach of your workspace to minimize disruptions during the painting process.

Protective Gear:

Wear protective gear such as gloves and aprons to shield your skin and clothing from paint spills and splashes.

If you're using silicone oil for creating cells in your pour paintings, consider wearing gloves to avoid direct contact with the oil.

Levelling Your Surface:

Ensure that your painting surface (canvas or board) is level to prevent the paint from pooling or running unevenly.

Use levelling tools such as a bubble level or adjustable easel to ensure a flat and even surface.

Prepping Your Canvas:

If you're using a canvas, make sure it's properly primed with gesso to create a smooth and absorbent surface for the paint.

If necessary, stretch and staple the canvas onto a stretcher frame to ensure it remains taut and flat during the pouring process.

Setting Up Workspace Access:

Arrange your workspace in a way that allows for easy access to your painting surface from all sides.

Consider placing your canvas on a raised surface or elevated platform to make it easier to manipulate and tilt during the pouring process.

Cleanup Supplies:

Keep a supply of paper towels, wet wipes, or rags handy for cleaning up spills, drips, and messes as you work.

Have a container of water or solvent available for rinsing brushes and tools between colours or after use.

By following these steps to prepare your workspace, you'll create a conducive environment for acrylic pour painting and minimize the risk of accidents or mishaps during the creative process.

Choose Your Pouring Technique:

There are various pouring techniques you can try, such as the flip cup method, the swipe technique, or the dirty pour. Research and experiment to find the one you like best.

Pour Your Paint:

Once your paint is mixed, pour it onto the canvas in whatever pattern or design you desire. You can pour multiple colours at once or layer them for different effects.

Tilt Your Canvas:

Carefully tilt your canvas in different directions to spread the paint and create interesting patterns. This is where the magic happens, as the colours blend and interact with each other.

Let It Dry:

Once you're happy with the way your painting looks, set it aside to dry completely. This may take several hours or even overnight, depending on the thickness of your paint layers.

Touch Up (Optional):

After your painting is dry, you can touch up any areas that you're not satisfied with using additional paint or a brush.

Seal Your Painting (Optional):

If you want to protect your painting and give it a glossy finish, you can apply a clear acrylic sealant once it's completely dry.

Display Your Artwork:

Once your painting is finished and sealed (if desired), you can display it proudly in your home or give it as a gift to someone special.

Remember, experimentation is key in acrylic pour painting. Don't be afraid to try new techniques and combinations of colours to create unique and beautiful artwork. Have fun and enjoy the process!

Chapter 2: Exploring colour and composition

Understanding acrylic paints and mediums is crucial for successful acrylic pour painting. Here's a breakdown of each:

1. Acrylic Paints:

Acrylic paints are water-based paints that dry quickly and are versatile in application. They come in a wide range of colours and consistencies, from fluid to heavy body.

When choosing acrylic paints for pour painting, consider the opacity, viscosity, and colour intensity of the paints. Fluid acrylics are commonly used because they have a thinner consistency, making them ideal for pouring techniques.

It's essential to use quality acrylic paints that contain high pigment loads for vibrant and long-lasting results.

2. Pouring Mediums:

Pouring mediums are additives that are mixed with acrylic paint to enhance flow, extend drying time, and improve adhesion. They also help to create the characteristic fluidity needed for pour painting.

There are various types of pouring mediums available, such as:

Liquitex Pouring Medium: A popular choice for acrylic pour artists, Liquitex Pouring Medium is designed specifically for creating fluid effects and maintaining colour intensity.

Floetrol: Often used as an alternative pouring medium, Floetrol is a paint additive that improves flow and levelling without affecting colour or bonding.

GAC (Golden Artist Colours) 800: Another option from Golden Artist Colours, GAC 800 is a pouring medium that dries with a glossy finish and maintains the integrity of the paint film.

Experimenting with different pouring mediums can help you achieve the desired consistency and effects in your pour paintings.

3. Water:

While pouring mediums are essential for achieving the desired fluidity in acrylic pour painting, water can also be used to thin acrylic paint and adjust its consistency. However, excessive use of water can weaken the paint film and affect adhesion, so it's best to use it sparingly.

4. Silicone Oil:

Silicone oil is often used in acrylic pour painting to create cells—round or irregularly shaped formations that occur when the silicone oil repels the paint, causing it to separate and form patterns.

Silicone oil should be used sparingly, as too much can cause excessive cell formation or interfere with the paint's drying process. It's essential to mix the silicone oil thoroughly into the paint mixture before pouring.

Understanding how acrylic paints and mediums interact with each other will enable you to control the flow, consistency, and appearance of your pour paintings. Experimentation and practice will help you find the right balance of materials to achieve your desired results.

Exploring colour and composition is an exciting aspect of acrylic pour painting that allows artists to create visually captivating and dynamic artworks. Here are some tips for experimenting with colour and composition in your pour paintings:

1. Colour Selection:

Choose a colour palette that evokes the mood or theme you want to convey in your painting. Consider the emotions and feelings associated with different colours and how they interact with each other.

Experiment with complementary, analogous, or contrasting colour schemes to create visual interest and harmony in your compositions.

Play with the opacity and intensity of your colours by mixing different ratios of paint and pouring mediums. Transparent and opaque colours can add depth and dimension to your paintings.

2. Colour Mixing:

Mix your acrylic paints with pouring mediums to achieve fluid and consistent consistency. Experiment with different ratios of paint to pouring medium to achieve the desired opacity and flow.

Try mixing colours directly on the canvas by pouring them in layers or blending them together using pouring techniques like the dirty pour or flip cup method.

Explore the effects of colour blending and layering as the paints interact with each other during the pouring process. Watch how colours merge and create new shades and tones as they flow across the canvas.

3. Composition Techniques:

Consider the placement and arrangement of colours within your composition. Experiment with different compositions, such as central focal points, asymmetrical balances, or radial designs.

Use negative space to enhance the visual impact of your pour paintings. Allow areas of the canvas to remain unpainted or lightly covered to create contrast and balance in your compositions.

Experiment with different pouring techniques, such as pouring from different heights, tilting the canvas at various angles, or combining multiple pouring methods to create dynamic and engaging compositions.

4. Adding Depth and Texture:

Incorporate additional elements into your pour paintings to add depth and texture. You can use tools like palette knives, brushes, or sponges to create texture effects or add details after the initial pouring process.

Experiment with layering techniques by pouring multiple layers of paint on top of each other to create depth and dimension in your compositions.

Consider adding embellishments such as glitter, metallic pigments, or other mixed media elements to enhance the visual interest of your paintings.

5. Practice and Experimentation:

The key to mastering colour and composition in acrylic pour painting is practice and experimentation. Don't be afraid to try new techniques, mix different colours, and explore various compositions to discover what works best for you.

Keep a sketchbook or journal to record your ideas, experiments, and observations. Take note of what you like and what you want to improve upon in your pour paintings.

By experimenting with colour and composition in acrylic pour painting, you can create stunning and expressive artworks that capture the imagination and evoke emotions in viewers. Allow yourself to explore and embrace the creative process, and let your intuition guide you as you unleash your artistic vision on the canvas.

Chapter 3: Advanced pouring techniques

Acrylic pour painting offers a variety of techniques that allow artists to create unique and captivating compositions. Here are some basic pouring techniques to get you started:

Dirty Pour:

The dirty pour technique involves mixing multiple colours of thinned acrylic paint and pouring them onto the canvas simultaneously from a single cup. Here's how to do it:

Prepare your acrylic paints by thinning them with a pouring medium to achieve a fluid consistency.

Layer the colours in a cup, alternating between different shades to create depth and interest.

Once the cup is filled, flip it upside down onto the canvas and lift it away to release the paint.

Tilt the canvas in different directions to spread the paint and create unique patterns and blends.

Flip Cup:

Similar to the dirty pour technique, the flip cup method involves pouring multiple colours of paint into a cup and then flipping it onto the canvas. Here's how to do it:

Prepare your acrylic paints as described above.

Pour each colour of paint into a single cup, layering them to create a stacked effect.

Place the canvas over the cup and flip them together so that the cup is upside down on the canvas.

Lift the cup away from the canvas to release the paint, then tilt the canvas to spread the paint and create patterns.

Swiping:

Swiping is a technique used to create linear patterns and cells in acrylic pour paintings. Here's how to do it:

Pour a base layer of thinned acrylic paint onto the canvas.

Pour additional colours of paint onto the canvas in a random pattern.

Use a tool such as a palette knife, spatula, or piece of cardboard to swipe through the wet paint, dragging the colours across the surface.

Experiment with different swiping motions and pressures to create varying effects.

String Pull:

The string pull technique involves dipping a piece of string or yarn into thinned acrylic paint and then dragging it across the canvas to create lines and patterns. Here's how to do it:

Dip a length of string or yarn into thinned acrylic paint, ensuring that it's fully coated.

Place one end of the string onto the canvas and gently drag it across the surface in a straight line or curving motion.

Lift the string away from the canvas to reveal the painted pattern.

Repeat the process with different colours and directions to create layered effects.

These are just a few basic pouring techniques to experiment with in acrylic pour painting. As you gain experience, feel free to combine techniques, adjust paint consistencies, and explore new methods to unleash your creativity and produce stunning works of art.

Advanced pouring techniques in acrylic pour painting allow artists to create intricate and captivating effects. Here are some advanced techniques to explore:

1. Dutch Pour:

The Dutch pour technique involves pouring multiple colors of thinned acrylic paint onto the canvas and then using a blow dryer, air compressor, or straw to manipulate the paint and create intricate patterns and designs.

Pour the paint onto the canvas in a random pattern, overlapping colors to create depth and interest.

Use the blow dryer or other tool to gently blow or push the paint across the canvas, allowing the colours to blend and create organic shapes and patterns.

Experiment with different speeds, angles, and distances to achieve varying effects, such as wispy veils of colour, intricate cells, or bold lines.

2. Resin Pour:

Resin pouring involves mixing acrylic paint with epoxy resin and pouring it onto the canvas to create a glossy, glass-like finish with vibrant colours and depth.

Mix the acrylic paint with the resin according to the manufacturer's instructions, ensuring proper ratios for optimal curing and adhesion.

Pour the resin mixture onto the canvas and spread it evenly using a spreader or brush.

Use a torch or heat gun to remove air bubbles and create a smooth surface.

Experiment with layering techniques by pouring multiple layers of resin, adding embellishments between layers, or embedding objects within the resin for added texture and visual interest.

3. Swipe and Drag Techniques:

Swipe and drag techniques involve using tools such as palette knives, combs, or squeegees to create linear patterns and textures in the paint.

Pour multiple colours of thinned acrylic paint onto the canvas in a random pattern.

Use a tool to swipe or drag through the wet paint, pulling the colours across the surface to create lines, waves, or other geometric shapes.

Experiment with different tools and techniques to achieve varying effects, such as fine lines, broad strokes, or intricate patterns.

4. Pouring on Different Surfaces:

Experiment with pouring acrylic paint onto different surfaces, such as wood panels, ceramic tiles, or glass, to create unique and versatile artworks.

Prepare the surface by priming or sealing it to ensure proper adhesion and durability.

Explore how the texture and absorbency of different surfaces affect the flow and appearance of the paint, and adapt your pouring techniques accordingly.

5. Sculptural Pouring:

Sculptural pouring techniques involve building up layers of acrylic paint on the canvas to create three-dimensional forms and textures.

Pour multiple layers of thinned acrylic paint onto the canvas, allowing each layer to dry partially before adding the next.

Use tools such as palette knives, spatulas, or your fingers to sculpt and manipulate the paint, creating raised areas, ridges, and textures.

Experiment with different layering techniques and additive materials, such as sand, fibres, or beads, to enhance the sculptural quality of your paintings.

These advanced pouring techniques in acrylic pour painting offer endless possibilities for experimentation and creative expression. As you explore these techniques, remember to embrace the unpredictable nature of pour painting and allow yourself to follow your intuition and artistic instincts. With practice and experimentation, you'll develop your own unique style and create stunning works of art that captivate and inspire.

Chapter 4: Trouble shooting and tips

Acrylic pour painting can be a wonderfully rewarding process, but it also comes with its own set of challenges. Here are some troubleshooting tips and general advice to help you navigate common issues and improve your pour painting technique:

1. Paint Consistency:

Issue: Paint is too thick or too thin, leading to poor flow and blending.

Solution: Experiment with different ratios of acrylic paint to pouring medium until you achieve the desired consistency. Aim for a consistency similar to warm honey for optimal flow.

2. Cell Formation:

Issue: Inconsistent or undesired cell formation in your pour painting.

Solution: Adjust the amount of silicone oil used in your paint mixture. Use a minimal amount of silicone oil and distribute it evenly throughout the paint to achieve more controlled cell formation. Additionally, try altering the density of your paint layers and experimenting with different pouring techniques to influence cell formation.

3. Cracking or Flaking:

Issue: Paint cracks or flakes after drying.

Solution: Ensure that your painting surface is properly prepared and primed with gesso to promote paint adhesion. Avoid overthinning your paint with pouring medium, as this can weaken the paint film and lead to cracking. Allow each layer of paint to dry completely before adding additional layers to prevent cracking.

4. Uneven Coverage:

Issue: Uneven coverage or pooling of paint on the canvas.

Solution: Level your painting surface before pouring to ensure even distribution of paint. Tilt the canvas gently in different directions to spread the paint evenly and prevent pooling. Use a palette knife or spatula to manipulate the paint and fill in any bare spots on the canvas.

5. Muddy Colours:

Issue: Colours blend together and become muddy or dull.

Solution: Be mindful of the colours you choose and how they interact with each other. Avoid overmixing your paint colours to prevent them from blending together too much. Consider using a limited colour palette and allowing each colour to shine on its own. Experiment with layering techniques and translucent colours to maintain colour vibrancy.

6. Drying Time:

Issue: Paint takes too long to dry, leading to extended wait times between layers or potential smudging.

Solution: Use acrylic paints with a fast drying time or add a drying accelerator to your paint mixture. Work in a well-ventilated area with adequate airflow to speed up the drying process. Avoid applying thick layers of paint, as this can prolong drying times.

7. Cleanup:

Issue: Difficulty cleaning up spilled or excess paint.

Solution: Keep a supply of wet wipes, paper towels, or rags on hand to quickly clean up spills and drips. Use a damp cloth or sponge to wipe down your work surface and tools after each painting session. Consider using disposable gloves to minimize mess and make cleanup easier.

By troubleshooting common issues and implementing these tips, you can enhance your acrylic pour painting technique and create stunning works of art with confidence and ease. Remember to embrace experimentation and enjoy the creative process!

Chapter : Finding your Style and Voice

Acrylic pour painting is such a versatile and exciting medium, offering endless possibilities for creativity. Discovering your unique style and voice within acrylic pouring is a journey of experimentation, exploration, and self-expression. Here are some steps to help you find your style and voice in acrylic pour painting:

Experiment with Techniques: Start by experimenting with different pouring techniques such as the flip cup, dirty pour, swipe, or Dutch pour. Each technique creates distinct effects, and through experimentation, you'll discover which ones resonate with you the most.

Play with Colour: Explore different colour combinations and observe how they interact with each other when poured onto the canvas. Consider the mood and atmosphere you want to evoke with your artwork and choose colours accordingly. Don't be afraid to mix your own custom colours to create unique palettes.

Develop Consistency: As you experiment with various techniques and colour combinations, you'll start to develop a consistent approach to your work. This consistency doesn't mean creating the same painting over and over again but rather finding elements or themes that define your style, whether it's a particular colour palette, texture, or composition.

Embrace Imperfections: Acrylic pouring is known for its unpredictable nature, and sometimes unexpected results can lead to the most interesting artworks. Embrace imperfections and accidents as part of the creative process, allowing them to inform and enrich your style rather than seeing them as mistakes to be corrected.

Find Inspiration: Look for inspiration not only within the acrylic pouring community but also from other art forms, nature, architecture, or everyday life. Pay attention to the elements that resonate with you and incorporate them into your own work in a way that feels authentic.

Express Yourself: Your style and voice in acrylic pour painting should ultimately be a reflection of your personality, emotions, and experiences. Don't be afraid to infuse your artwork with your unique perspective and voice, whether it's through bold colour choices, dynamic compositions, or subtle details.

Practice, Practice, Practice: Like any other art form, finding your style and voice in acrylic pour painting takes time and practice. Keep experimenting, learning from both successes and failures, and trust that with dedication, your distinctive style will emerge and evolve over time.

Remember, the journey of finding your style and voice in acrylic pour painting is a deeply personal and ongoing process. Enjoy the exploration, embrace the journey, and celebrate the uniqueness of your creative expression.

Congratulations! You've reached the end of our journey through the colourful world of acrylic pour painting. Armed with newfound knowledge and inspiration, you're ready to unleash your creativity and create stunning works of art that reflect your unique style and vision.

Remember, acrylic pour painting is as much about the process as it is about the final result. So, embrace experimentation, trust your instincts, and most importantly, have fun! Whether you're creating art for yourself or sharing it with the world, may your journey be filled with endless creativity and boundless possibilities.

Happy pouring!

www.ingramcontent.com/pod-product-compliance
Lightning Source LLC
Chambersburg PA
CBHW062210220526
45470CB00009B/2995